HILLARY CLINTON

Katie Kawa

PowerKiDS
press

New York

Published in 2017 by The Rosen Publishing Group, Inc.
29 East 21st Street, New York, NY 10010

First Edition

Editor: Katie Kawa
Book Design: Reann Nye

Photo Credits: Cover, pp. 1, 3–18, 20–29, 30–32 (halftone pattern) Solomin Andrey/Shutterstock.com; cover, p. 1 Win McNamee/Getty Images News/Getty Images; p. 5 Adam Bettcher/Getty Images News/ Getty Images; p. 6 Steve Kagan/The LIFE Images Collection/Getty Images; p. 7 SAUL LOEB/ AFP/Getty Images; p. 9 Lee Balterman/The LIFE Picture Collection/Getty Images; p. 10 Pool/ Getty Images News/Getty Images; p. 11 BRENDAN SMIALOWSKI/AFP/Getty Images; p. 12 Kevin Winter/Getty Images Entertainment/Getty Images; p. 13 Theo Westenberger/ Hulton Archive/Getty Images; p. 15 JOYCE NALTCHAYAN/AFP/Getty Images; p. 17 Esther Horvath/ FilmMagic/Getty Images; p. 19 Jemal Countess/WireImage/Getty Images; p. 21 TIMOTHY A. CLARY/ AFP/Getty Images; p. 23 Paula Bronstein/Getty Images News/Getty Images; p. 25 DON EMMERT/ AFP/Getty Images; pp. 27, 30 Bloomberg/Getty Images; p. 29 Isaac Brekken/Getty Images News/ Getty Images.

Library of Congress Cataloging-in-Publication Data

Kawa, Katie.
 Hillary Clinton / Katie Kawa.
    pages cm. — (Superwomen role models)
 Includes index.
 ISBN 978-1-5081-4835-7 (pbk.)
 ISBN 978-1-5081-4773-2 (6 pack)
 ISBN 978-1-5081-4806-7 (library binding)
 1. Clinton, Hillary Rodham—Juvenile literature. 2. Presidents' spouses—United States—Biography—Juvenile literature. 3. Women cabinet officers—United States—Biography—Juvenile literature. 4. Cabinet officers— United States—Biography—Juvenile literature. 5. United States. Department of State—Biography—Juvenile literature. 6. Women legislators—United States—Biography—Juvenile literature. 7. Legislators—United States—Biography—Juvenile literature. 8. Women presidential candidates—United States—Biography— Juvenile literature. 9. Presidential candidates—United States—Biography—Juvenile literature. I. Title.
 E887.C55K39 2017
 327.730092—dc23
 [B]
                              2015034128

Manufactured in the United States of America

CPSIA Compliance Information: Batch #BS16PK: For Further Information contact Rosen Publishing, New York, New York at 1-800-237-9932

CONTENTS

MAKING A NAME
FOR HERSELF

In 1992, Hillary Clinton was known mainly as the wife of presidential candidate Bill Clinton. While campaigning for her husband that year, she said of herself, "Our lives are a mixture of different roles. Most of us are doing the best we can to find whatever the right balance is….For me, that balance is family, work, and service." As people have learned more about Hillary, they've learned that she's devoted her life to those three areas. Her family, her career, and her ability to serve others continue to be as important to her now as they were in 1992.

Today, Hillary is known as much more than just President Bill Clinton's wife. She's made a name for herself as a public servant, reaching new heights for a woman in the political world.

Hillary Clinton has held many titles during her time in the political spotlight, including First Lady, senator, secretary of state, and presidential candidate. She's set a strong example of leadership and service to her country throughout her career.

GROWING UP

Hillary Clinton was born Hillary Diane Rodham on October 26, 1947. She was the oldest of three children, with two younger brothers, Hugh and Tony. Hillary grew up in Park Ridge, Illinois, which is near Chicago. Her father, Hugh, owned a **drapery** business, and the whole family would pitch in to help with it. Hillary's mother, Dorothy, started supporting herself at 14 years old after a difficult childhood. The tough times Hillary's mother faced in her youth **inspired** Hillary to devote much of her energy in her career to the needs of children.

Hillary's parents taught her to work hard, especially in school. Hillary was also active in her church. From a young age, she was interested in politics and social issues such as civil rights.

HILLARY'S CHILDHOOD HOME

Hillary's parents encouraged her to do well in school and to follow whatever career path she wanted to choose. Following their example, Hillary has worked hard to fight for better educational opportunities for young people in the United States and around the world.

A LEADER AND A LAWYER

Hillary combined her passion for politics with her love of learning in 1965, when she began studying political science at Wellesley College in Massachusetts. During her time at Wellesley, she served as a leader in student government, and she was asked to deliver a speech at her **commencement** in 1969.

After graduating from Wellesley, Hillary enrolled at Yale Law School in Connecticut. While in law school, Hillary grew even more interested in issues affecting children. Her passion for this cause was supported by Marian Wright Edelman, who is a lawyer and children's rights **advocate** who **mentored** Hillary.

Hillary graduated from Yale Law School in 1973. She was one of only 27 women in her graduating class of 235 students. One of her fellow students at Yale Law School was her future husband, Bill Clinton.

IN HER WORDS

"The challenge now is to practice politics as the art of making what appears to be impossible, possible."
Wellesley College commencement address, delivered in 1969

This photograph was taken as part of a 1969 *Life* magazine story about student leaders in U.S. colleges. Hillary was featured along with four other student leaders who delivered the commencement addresses at their colleges.

LIFE AFTER LAW SCHOOL

Although Hillary and Bill had grown close during their time at Yale Law School, she chose not to follow him back to his home state of Arkansas immediately following graduation. She also chose not to pursue a high-paying career at a major law firm in a big city. Instead, she worked for the Children's Defense Fund in Massachusetts. She chose to continue to fight for **underserved** children, and she spent a lot of time working to improve education for children with disabilities.

BILL AND HILLARY

Bill Clinton met Hillary Rodham when they were both students at Yale Law School. They were both interested in politics and social issues, and they soon began spending much of their time together. After spending time apart as they pursued their career goals following graduation, they were married on October 11, 1975. Bill and Hillary's shared political ideals and interests have made them good partners in politics. They've supported each other's career goals throughout their marriage.

Improving the lives of children has been important to Hillary from her earliest days as a lawyer, and it continues to be important to her today.

In 1974, Hillary served as a lawyer for the committee looking into the possible **impeachment** of President Richard Nixon. When Nixon resigned later that year, Hillary chose to move to Arkansas to be with Bill. A new stage of her life was about to begin.

ACHIEVEMENTS IN ARKANSAS

When Hillary moved to Arkansas, she took a job teaching at the University of Arkansas Law School. She later worked for the Rose Law Firm, which is a major law firm in Little Rock, Arkansas. Hillary eventually became the first woman to be named a **full partner** at this law firm.

In 1978, Bill was elected governor of Arkansas. Hillary balanced her duties as the state's First Lady with her legal career and her family. In 1980, Hillary and Bill became parents to a daughter, Chelsea.

RAISING A ROLE MODEL

Hillary's work ethic and desire to help others set a good example for her only daughter. Chelsea studied at some of the best schools in the world, receiving degrees from Stanford University, Columbia University, and the University of Oxford. Chelsea currently works for the Bill, Hillary & Chelsea Clinton Foundation, which is a charitable organization started by her parents. She has a special interest in improving global health, and she's also devoted much of her energy to the needs of women and girls around the world.

CHELSEA CLINTON

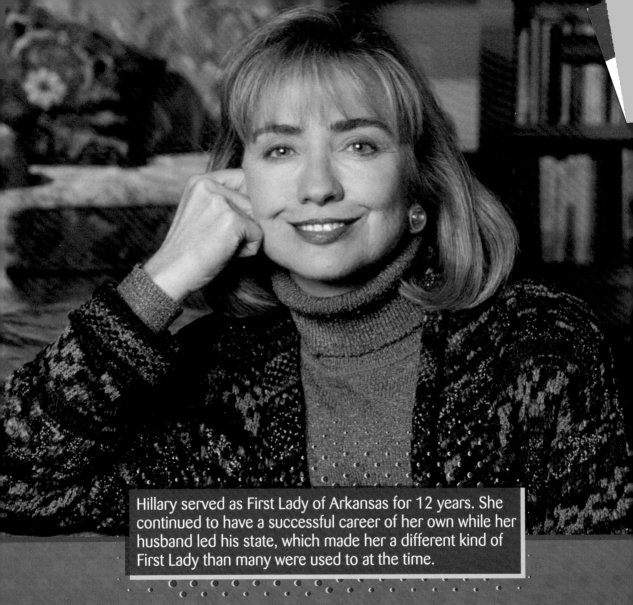

Hillary served as First Lady of Arkansas for 12 years. She continued to have a successful career of her own while her husband led his state, which made her a different kind of First Lady than many were used to at the time.

As the First Lady of Arkansas, Hillary worked to improve health care for the people in the state who were living in poverty. Education also continued to be a cause close to Hillary's heart. She even served as the chair, or leader, of the Arkansas Education Standards Committee.

A NEW KIND OF FIRST LADY

In 1992, Bill Clinton was elected president of the United States, and he was re-elected in 1996. Hillary wasn't a traditional First Lady. She took an active role in creating new government policies and programs. Hillary even had her own office in the West Wing of the White House, which is where the president's offices are located. This was a first for a First Lady of the United States.

Hillary was especially active in matters of health care reform. She helped give children living in poverty access to health insurance. Hillary also dedicated time and resources to helping other women during her years as First Lady of the United States. She was a major force behind the creation of the Department of Justice's Office on Violence Against Women.

IN HER WORDS

"Whether I am meant to or not, I challenge assumptions about women. I do make some people uncomfortable, which I'm well aware of, but that's just part of coming to grips with what I believe is still one of the most important pieces of unfinished business in human history—empowering women to be able to stand up for themselves."

Interview with *Vogue* magazine, published in November 2009

Some people didn't like how active Hillary was in policy making during her husband's time in the White House. However, she didn't let that stop her from doing what she could to help people, especially children and women.

FIGHTING FOR WOMEN'S RIGHTS

Hillary has spoken out about women's rights on many occasions throughout her political career. However, one of her most groundbreaking speeches on this topic came in 1995 during a trip to Beijing, China. Beijing was the site of the United Nations (UN) Fourth World Conference on Women. During this meeting of **activists** and world leaders, the Beijing Declaration and Platform for Action was adopted by 189 countries. This document laid out plans for gender equality and empowering women around the world.

At this conference, Hillary spoke about the problems facing women around the world. She also spoke about what could be done to help gender equality become a reality. This conference was a turning point in the worldwide fight for women's rights, and Hillary played a big part in its success.

IN HER WORDS

"If there is one message that echoes forth from this conference, it is that human rights are women's rights...and women's rights are human rights."
Speech to the UN Fourth World Conference on Women in Beijing, China, delivered on September 5, 1995

In 2015, Hillary joined other activists and leaders to celebrate the 20th anniversary of the UN Fourth World Conference on Women. That historic conference addressed issues in 12 major areas still studied today, such as women and the media, violence against women, and women and health.

SERVING IN THE SENATE

Hillary's political career didn't end when her husband left the White House. In fact, that was when her career started to take off. Near the end of Bill's second term as president, he and Hillary bought a house in New York State. Hillary then ran for U.S. Senate in New York, becoming the first U.S. First Lady to run for national political office. In 2000, Hillary was elected to the U.S. Senate, and she was reelected in 2006. Hillary was the first female senator from New York.

During her time in the Senate, Hillary worked on legislation geared toward her areas of interest, including health care and children's issues. She also served on important committees during her two terms as a senator, including the Committee on Armed Services.

Hillary's time as a senator showed that she could have a successful political career of her own after her husband stepped out of the national spotlight.

RUNNING FOR PRESIDENT

In 2007, Hillary announced the next big step in her political career: She was running for president. It was her dream to be the first female president of the United States. Hillary was an early leader in the race to be the Democratic Party's candidate in the 2008 presidential election. She won more **primaries** than any woman who had ever run for president before.

While Hillary experienced successes during her campaign, she remained locked in a tight battle with Barack Obama, who was a senator from Illinois at that time. Ultimately, Hillary couldn't beat Senator Obama, who would go on to become president. Although she didn't achieve her goal in 2008, Hillary proved to many Americans that a woman could be taken seriously as a presidential candidate.

IN HER WORDS

"Although we weren't able to shatter that highest, hardest glass ceiling this time, thanks to you, it's got about 18 million cracks in it…and the light is shining through like never before, filling us all with the hope and the sure knowledge that the path will be a little easier next time."

Speech delivered to supporters in Washington, D.C., on June 7, 2008

Millions of people supported Hillary during her 2008 presidential campaign, showing that people were more open to the idea of a female president than ever before.

SECRETARY OF STATE

President Obama knew that Hillary's political knowledge and experience could help him during his time in the White House. In 2009, Hillary became secretary of state. By taking this position, Hillary became the head of the State Department, which is responsible for foreign affairs. Hillary was the first former First Lady to serve as a member of a president's cabinet, or group of executive advisers.

Hillary was known as a successful secretary of state. She worked hard to improve relationships between the United States and other countries around the world. Hillary visited more countries than any secretary of state before her. She traveled to 112 different countries before she stepped down from the position in 2013.

IN HER WORDS

"Always aim high, work hard, and care deeply about what you believe in. And, when you stumble, keep faith. And, when you're knocked down, get right back up, and never listen to anyone who says you can't or shouldn't go on."

Speech delivered to supporters in Washington, D.C., on June 7, 2008

Hillary and President Obama fought against each other on the campaign trail, but they formed a strong working relationship during her time as secretary of state. They set a good example of putting your differences aside and working together for the common good.

NO CEILINGS

Even after Hillary left the State Department in 2013, she continued to serve others both in the United States and around the world. She became a more active force in the Bill, Hillary & Chelsea Clinton Foundation. This foundation aims to help those in need through many different programs in areas such as global health, economic development, and health and wellness.

Helping girls and women is another important part of Hillary's work with the foundation. She's the driving force behind No Ceilings: The Full Participation Project, which is an effort to study and share the progress made since the UN Fourth World Conference on Women. Hillary and Chelsea are working together on this project to help empower women around the world.

TOO SMALL TO FAIL

Hillary has never stopped working to improve the lives of children in the United States. In 2013, she launched a project called Too Small to Fail, which was created to help children from birth to age five. The goal of Too Small to Fail is to promote scientific research on early childhood development. With this research, adults will have a better understanding of how to raise healthy children who are ready to learn by the time they start school.

The Full Participatio

CEILIN

Hillary and Chelsea teamed up with Melinda Gates (left) to launch No Ceilings: The Full Participation Project. Melinda is another women's rights activist who's devoted her life to helping others.

WHAT'S NEXT?

In 2014, Hillary took on another new title: grandmother. That year, Chelsea had a daughter of her own, Charlotte Clinton Mezvinsky. Hillary has said that having a granddaughter has made her think even more about the future of women in the United States and around the world.

Being a grandmother didn't mean it was time for Hillary to start slowing down, though. She continued her work with her family's foundation, but she also discovered she wasn't quite ready to leave politics behind. In April 2015, Hillary announced that she was once again running for president.

WRITING HER STORY

In 1996, Hillary wrote her first book while serving as First Lady of the United States. Called *It Takes a Village: And Other Lessons Children Teach Us*, this book describes Hillary's view of what it takes to raise healthy and happy children. In 2003, Hillary published *Living History*, in which she told the story of her time in the White House. Hillary also wrote a book about her experiences as secretary of state. This book, which is titled *Hard Choices*, was published in 2014.

Hillary announced she was running for president again through a video that was released on YouTube.

As she began campaigning for the 2016 presidential election, Hillary continued to speak out about the causes that have meant the most to her throughout her life, including equality for all Americans and improving the quality of life for the next generation of citizens.

A STRONG EXAMPLE

Hillary Clinton has never stopped fighting for what's important to her. From her days as a student to her time as secretary of state, she's worked hard to make the world a better place.

Hillary has blazed new trails for women in the world of American politics. She redefined the role of the First Lady by taking an active role in politics both during and after her husband's terms as president.

Hillary also showed the world that if you believe in something, you should never give up. She didn't let her loss during the 2008 presidential campaign stop her from running again. Hillary's attitude that anyone—especially a woman—can do anything they set their mind to makes her a superwoman role model.

Hillary has shown that leadership ability doesn't depend on gender. She's never let the fact that she's a woman stop her from taking on new challenges, and that sets a strong example for the next generation of female leaders.

IN HER WORDS

"You have just one life to live. It is yours. Own it, claim it, live it, do the best you can with it."
Interview with *Marie Claire* magazine from October 2012

TIMELINE

October 26, 1947: Hillary Diane Rodham is born in Park Ridge, Illinois.

1965: Hillary begins studying at Wellesley College.

1969: Hillary delivers the commencement address at her graduation from Wellesley, and she begins studying at Yale Law School.

1973: Hillary graduates from Yale Law School.

October 11, 1975: Hillary marries Bill Clinton.

1978: Bill is elected governor of Arkansas, making Hillary the state's First Lady.

1980: Hillary gives birth to a daughter, Chelsea.

1992: Hillary becomes First Lady of the United States when Bill is elected president.

1995: Hillary speaks at the UN Fourth World Conference on Women.

2000: Hillary is elected to the U.S. Senate.

2007: Hillary announces she's running for president.

2009: Hillary becomes President Barack Obama's secretary of state.

April 2015: Hillary announces she's running for president in the 2016 election.

GLOSSARY

activist: Someone who acts strongly in support of or against an issue.

advocate: A person who argues for or supports a cause or policy.

commencement: A ceremony during which degrees or diplomas are given to students who have graduated from a college.

drapery: Cloth coverings that hang in loose folds.

full partner: A person who is jointly responsible for a business, such as a law firm, with others in their partnership.

impeachment: To charge a public official with a crime done while in office.

inspire: To move someone to do something great.

mentor: To teach, give guidance, or give advice to someone, especially a less experienced person.

primary: An election in which members of the same political party run against each other for the chance to be in a larger and more important election.

underserved: Not given access to certain important services, such as health and social services.

INDEX

WEBSITES

Due to the changing nature of Internet links, PowerKids Press has developed an
online list of websites related to the subject of this book. This site is updated regularly.
Please use this link to access the list: www.powerkidslinks.com/sprwmn/clntn